H. P. Danks

Zanie

An operetta

H. P. Danks

Zanie
An operetta

ISBN/EAN: 9783337315559

Printed in Europe, USA, Canada, Australia, Japan

Cover: Foto ©Thomas Meinert / pixelio.de

More available books at **www.hansebooks.com**

ZANIE

AN OPERETTA.

LIBRETTO BY

FANNY CROSBY,

MUSIC BY

H. P. DANKS.

CINCINNATI:

Published by The **JOHN CHURCH CO.,** 74 W. Fourth Street.

CHICAGO:

Root & Sons Music Co.

200 Wabash Avenue.

NEW YORK:

The J. Church Co..

19 East 16th Street.

PRINCIPAL VOICES.

ZANIE, *Soprano.*
MRS. RINGGOLD, *Soprano.*
EMILY, *Soprano.*
HEPSICHORE, *Contralto.*
STELLA, *Contralto.*

HERBERT, *Tenor.*
SIR HENRY, *Baritone.*
MR. RINGGOLD, *Baritone.*
FARRAL, *Basso.*

REMARKS.

1. ACCOMPANIMENT.—Where an orchestra is impracticable, a Piano-forte alone or Piano and Organ will make an effective accompaniment for this operetta.

2. SCENERY.—Only three scenes are really necessary : A Forest, Garden, and Drawing-room. Where there are no convenieces for the Forest and Garden scenes, improvise them the best that circumstances will allow. Where this can not be done, the audience will have to imagine the stage a forest, garden, etc. A drawing-room can be made almost anywhere.

3. PROPERTIES.—A kettle of some sort, suspended upon sticks or stones, over a seeming fire, for Hepsichore, in Scene VI.

A Chair placed upon a box covered with carpeting will answer for the Queen's Pedestal, in Scene VI.

A Tent of some kind will be required for Zanie, in Scene VI.

Also, two or three more for the Gipsy outfit, in Scenes I, III, and VI, if possible.

In place of an extra Piano-forte for Stella, in Scene V, a small Organ, or even a Table will answer the purpose, as it is not necessary that Stella's exercise should be heard, and Emily's Solo (No. 10) is accompanied by the same person or persons that accompany the whole Operetta.

4. The Chorus following Herbert's Solo (No. 14) would be most effective if rendered by voices invisible (back of the scenes or in an adjoining room) by such persons as are not required on the stage at the time.

5. Solo (No. 16) may be sung (all three verses) by one Gipsy (a Soprano), or by three different Sopranos, or two different Sopranos and one Tenor.

6. NUMBER OF PERFORMERS.—Of course it is optional as to the number of people taking part in the Operetta. The greater the number of Gipsies (who do the principal part of the choruses), the more effective the choruses will be.

The Gipsies, having previously disappeared from the scene as such, will, with a change in their make-up, become part of the company of guests and friends of the Glenvilles, who precede the bridal party from the Chapel to the Mansion, and sing the Wedding Chorus (No. 19).

The number of young ladies accompanying Irene (in Scene IV), including Emily and Florence, must be six at least, and twelve or more if convenient, as they are divided into Choruses (Nos. 8 and 9).

7. COSTUMES.—It will be seen by glancing over the Libretto that there is very little required in the way of elaborate Costumes. Zanie must be dressed at first in white, with a wreath of flowers on her head; afterwards as a bride, etc.

Hepsichore, Farral, and the rest of the gipsies must be made up as typical gipsies. The men should wear high boots to the knee, dark-colored pants, cutaway jackets, wool shirts, felt and straw hats (large). All the gipsies may be adorned with a plenty of showy jewelry. etc. The women dress in gay-colored woolen dresses, fancy-colored calico aprons, made long, flats, trimmed or not (for old women, calico bonnets), low shoes and gay stockings, etc., etc.

All other characters are dressed as occasion requires in ordinary society. Of course, much depends upon the taste and convenience of the different persons taking leading parts as to how they make themselves up. By reading over the Libretto they can get as fair an idea of what their make-up should be as we can advise.

ZANIE.

AN OPERETTA.

Characters.

No. 1. INTRODUCTION.

SCENE I.—*A Gypsy Camp in the outskirts of Devonshire, England. The Gypsies are making preparations for a hasty removal. In the midst of these preparations they sing—*

No. 2. CHORUS.

The dew is on the snow-white thorn,
The owl has gone to rest,
And waning stars are bearing hence
The hours we love the best;
Now soars the lark on airy wing,
To hail the opening day,
Come, strike our tents with lively hands,
We gypsies must away.

Bring forth, bring forth our grazing steeds,
Let all be quickly done,
For we must reach our destined place,
Ere sets the golden sun;
'Tis gleaming o'er the mountain top,
With bright and genial ray,
Come, strike our tents with lively hands,
We gypsies must away.

There's game for us and well we know
'Tis won by stealth and care,
And he who best can play his part,
Will win the largest share:
Good-bye, good-bye, ye forest wilds
And smiling vales so gay,
Keep watch for us till our return,
We gypsies must away. .

SCENE II.—*A Room in an elegant Mansion, the residence of* SIR HENRY GLENVILLE *and his family, situated near a large country town.* STELLA, *the daughter, sits by the window reading.*

Enter HERBERT, *her brother, in great excitement.*

HERBERT. Stella! Stella! I have been looking all over for you, and at last here you are, devouring the pages of that old volume with the eagerness of a sage or philosopher.

STELLA. Why, Bertie, what has happened? Your cheeks are flushed, and you are nearly out of breath. Sit down quietly and tell all about it.

HERBERT. A band of real gypsies have just arrived in the neighborhood, and are preparing for a grand merrymaking. Their encampment is only a mile and a half distant, and papa says, if we like, there will be no harm in our taking a look at them.

STELLA. Is it the same party who were here some ten or twelve months ago, and who created such an excitement among the peasantry?

HERBERT. Yes; and the same maiden who attracted so much attention among the gentry, and with whom I had the good fortune to become acquainted, is still with them. Oh, Stella! Zanie is a most lovable character, and has a voice like a nightingale.

STELLA. Why, Herbert Glenville, how can you apply the word lovable to anyone belonging to a people so utterly destitute of culture and refinement! I agree with you that some of their women are possessed of great beauty, but in this particular instance it seems to me that your enthusiasm carries you far beyond your judgment. (3)

HERBERT. Are you willing to believe the evidence of your own eyes?

STELLA. Certainly I am!

HERBERT. Then don your hat and feathers and other trappings, and let us go to the camp. Make haste, please; we have not a moment to lose.

SCENE III.—*The same Encampment. The Gypsies arrange themselves in a group.* HERBERT *and* STELLA *stand at a little distance, watching them.*

No. 3. SOLO AND CHORUS OF GIPSIES.

SOLO.

Now begins our nightly revel,
Now amidst the dance we stand,
Who so gladsome, free and merry,
As a roving gypsy band?

CHORUS.

We will dance till high above us
Birds awake their matin chime,
Rural songs of mirth and pleasure,
With our footsteps keeping time.

SOLO.

Let the miser count his treasure,
Let the farmer till the soil,
Yet to labor we are strangers—
We were never made for toil.

CHORUS.

We will dance, etc.

SOLO.

Hip! hurrah! the moon is rising,
See, she comes, our sports to grace,
Peeping through the leafy branches,
With a mild approving face.

CHORUS.

We will dance, etc.

STELLA. Bertie, I am afraid to come in contact with these rude men and women. I have been told that they live by plunder, and who knows but they will rob and then take us prisoners?

HERBERT. Nonsense, you little goose! They will do nothing of the sort. Come along! There's Zanie. See! she is dressed in white, with a wreath of flowers on her head. Now gaze earnestly for a moment and tell me what you think of her. She is even more angelic than when I last saw her.

STELLA. You are quite right: she is indeed angelic; but she is no gypsy, I assure you.

HERBERT. What?

STELLA. She is no gypsy; neither in form, feature or complexion does she bear the slightest resemblance to any of them.

HERBERT. Hush! she is aware of our presence and is coming to bid us welcome.

ZANIE *approaches and sings.*

No. 4. SOLO.

You are welcome, friends, to our greenwood home,
In the sylvan wilds where we love to roam,
We have spread our feast neath the wailing trees,
And our cheeks are fanned by the laughing breeze.

You are welcome, friends, to our festive cheer,
There is nought to harm, there is nought to fear,

Then, away, away to the dance to-night,
Let your hearts be gay, as your eyes are bright.

Yes! away, away to the dance with me,
I will bring you sweets from the honey bee,
I will gather fruits that are rich and rare,
And balmy breath from the roses fair.

STELLA (*aside to* HERBERT). What a charming voice! If she could only be induced to abandon this mode of life, she would make a fortune and become an ornament to society.

No. 5. DUO.—ZANIE AND HERBERT.

HERBERT.   Fly, Oh birdling, do not stay,
            Turn from gipsy life away,
            You should learn to spell and read,
            Will you not my counsel heed?

ZANIE.   Take this promise now, from me;
            If a gipsy you will be,
            Then your counsel I will heed;
            You shall teach me how to read.

HERBERT.   Will you be my faithful friend,
            May I on your word depend,
            Shall I find you ever true,
            What you promise, will you do?

ZANIE.   I will be your faithful friend,
            On my word you may depend,
            You shall find me ever true,
            What I promise, I will do.

No. 6. TRIO.—ZANIE, STELLA AND HERBERT.

Good-night, good-night, 'tis passing sweet,
Our friends in scenes like this to meet,
And though we now must say adieu,
We'll keep their mem'ry warm and true,
And should we meet another day,
Our steps as light, our hearts as gay,
Oh, may our friendship stronger grow—
But now, good-night! 'tis time to go!

ZANIE (*to* STELLA). Your pardon, lady; but your hair has accidentally escaped from beneath the comb which held it, and the comb is broken. If you will come with me for a moment, I will supply its place with another.

HERBERT. Go with her at once, Stella, and I will wait here until you return.   [*Exeunt* ZANIE *and* STELLA.

FARRAL (*a Gypsy, to* HERBERT). Halloo, my fine fellow! so you have not forgotten Zanie.

HERBERT. That would be quite impossible, sir.

FARRAL. Did you ever tell your father of your friendship for her, and your frequent visits to the gypsies?

HERBERT. I only told him of your arrival to-day, and obtained his permission to enjoy your evening festivities; but of my other visits he knows nothing, nor would I enlighten him for the world.

FARRAL. Hearken, my lad: The best thing for you is to run away and become one of us. Zanie and you would be companions to each other; and, besides, with a little training, I think we should be able to make a man of you. What do you think of it, eh?

HERBERT. Your proposition strikes me favorably; but I must have more time to consider upon it. It is not so easy to leave one's parents and home. (*Aside:*) If I can get Stella's promise to keep my secret, I'll run away this very night. Here she comes. Good-night, Farral! Good-night, all! I'll see you to-morrow.

No. 7. CHORUS OF GYPSIES.—MALE VOICES.

A jovial life is ours, Ha, ha!
With little of trouble or sorrow,
The clouds of to-day all vanish away
And bring us a brighter to-morrow, Ha, ha!
The proud may rest on their beds of down,
But we every house-dweller scorning,
Like birds on the wing will merrily sing,
And dance 'till the blush of the morning, Ha, ha!

Ah, gayly we roam the world, Ha, ha!
As free as the zephyr above us,
We frown on the cold, but honor the bold,
And smile to the darlings that love us; Ha, ha!
We watch the fields when the grain is ripe,
We look on the reapers that bind it,
We stay not to plead, but take what we need,
Wherever at night we may find it, Ha, ha!

SCENE IV.—*A Garden near* SIR HENRY'S *Residence.*

Enter STELLA *and* HERBERT.

HERBERT. Stella, do you love your brother sufficiently to keep whatever secret he may confide to you, without betraying him under any circumstances?

STELLA. Yes! But I hope you have done nothing wrong.

HERBERT. It is not what I have done, but what I intend to do. The truth is, I have a strange interest in the fate of that gypsy girl. I am anxious to do her good, and for that purpose, now that I have seen you safely home, I shall return to the camp and become a gypsy.

STELLA. Oh, Herbert, this is dreadful! It will break our hearts; I am sure it will. But I have promised, and will keep my word.

HERBERT. You're a dear, good girl. Now, good-bye! Don't fret about me; I'll come back again some day, and perhaps I will bring Zanie with me. (*Kisses* STELLA *and departs.*)

SCENE V.—*A Drawing-room in the Mansion.* STELLA *at the piano-forte, trying to remember a lesson, which she at last succeeds in playing with tolerable correctness.*

Enter IRENE (*an elder sister), accompanied by several of her associates (ladies).*

IRENE (*to* STELLA). I am pleased with the manner in which you have played the exercise I gave you, but such music is rather monotonous. Suppose you resign the piano to me, and you will join us in singing some of our favorite songs. Come, girls; what shall we sing first?

EMILY. Let us sing our song to the fairies, and its reply.

STELLA. Then we will divide ourselves in this way: one half of our number, embracing the largest of us, shall sing, "Tell us, fairies, where you dwell," and then the remaining half shall personate the fairies. Now, are you ready? Sing!

No. 8. THREE-PART CHORUS.—FEMALE VOICES.

Oh, tell us, fairies, where you dwell,
When winter winds are blowing,
When not a leaf is in the dell,
Nor brook or rill are flowing?
Where hide ye, then, Oh, mystic train?
In some bright star above us,
To whisper o'er the charm again,
That binds to those that love us?

Oh, tell us, fairies, where you dwell,
When snow-flakes crest the mountain,
When sylvan chimes no longer swell,
And frost has sealed the fountain;

Say! do ye plunge beneath the waves
In bells where moonbeams shining,
Reflect their light on coral caves,
Where nymphs their wreaths are twining?

STELLA. Now, fairies, to your places, and give us your answer.

No. 9. CHORUS OF FAIRIES.

We come from fairy land,
And roam where'er we will;
We heed not winter's chilling storms,
For we are happy still.
We roam the earth, the air,
And o'er the distant sea,
We visit every sunny clime,
Where'er our thoughts would be.

We scale the mountain's peak,
And sometimes in a star
We float away at dewy eve
To worlds unseen and far;
When gentle spring returns,
And May bells sweetly ring,
We seek the cool and shady grot
With forest sprites we sing.

IRENE. Now for a song. What shall it be; and who shall sing it?

FLORENCE. Emily has just learned a song which is entirely new. It has such a pretty name! It's called "Think of the absent one."

ALL. Oh, Emily! you will sing it for us, won't you?

EMILY. I will do my best.

IRENE. One moment! Here comes papa; he is very fond of music, and I know he will be pleased, as well as ourselves.

Enter SIR HENRY.

SIR HENRY. I can not allow you to enjoy all this sweet music alone, so I venture to intrude, and become your auditor.

IRENE. No intrusion whatever, papa, you are always welcome. Now, Emily,

EMILY *sings.*

No. 10. SOLO.

Think of the absent one gone from our sight,
Think of the absent one roaming to-night,
Lonely the heart may be, laden with care,
Think of the absent one, breathe him a prayer.

Think of the absent one, where has he gone?
Now at the vesper time comes not his song,
Far from his place of birth, chance on the main—
Bear him, ye gentle winds, home, home again.

SIR HENRY. How singular that you should have selected this song! And now, my friends, let me tell you of another strange event, which has affected me very deeply. A few hours ago I was waited upon by a gentleman from the United States, who is in search of his young daughter. She was stolen from her home at an early age, and her father has every reason to believe that she was brought to England, and he has come hither with the hope that he may be able to find her among the gypsies.

STELLA (*rising and bursting into tears*). Oh, papa, I must unburden my heart to you! My brother! my brother!

SIR HENRY. What of your brother, Stella?

STELLA. He has run away with the gypsies to the old forest.

IRENE (*angrily*). Why, Stella, you naughty, wicked girl! Have we not been taught never to be disobedient to the will of our parents? How dare you keep such a secret, when you know papa was always adverse to his having anything to do with this lawless people! You deserve to be severely punished—indeed you do!

SIR HENRY. Though Stella has erred, yet I believe she is really penitent ; and now it is your sympathy she needs, not your frowns, my daughter. Remember that while we are just, we should also be merciful. If my boy has gone, I must follow him immediately.   [*Exeunt all.*

SCENE VI.—*The Gypsy Camp in the Old Forest.* HEPSICHORE (*the pretended mother of* ZANIE, *and a fortune-teller*) *standing in her tent, throwing a mixture of drugs into a cauldron, which she stirs, and sings.*

No. 11. SOLO.

While the burning embers glow,
In the cauldron now I throw,
And together stir them well,
Drugs by whose mysterious spell
Past and future I can tell—
What has been, and what will be.
I to youthful lovers show
Fate and fortune, bliss and woe.
Now the magic drugs unite—
Now the liquid drops are bright.

Enter ZANIE *and* HERBERT *with their books, singing.*

No. 12. DUO.

BOTH.   'Tis joy, 'tis joy, 'tis joy to learn to spell and read—
           To learn to spell and read.
ZANIE.   My thanks to you for all.
HERBERT.   No thanks to me at all.
ZANIE.   Yes, thanks to you for all.
HERBERT.   No thanks at all.
ZANIE.   My thanks to you for all.
HERBERT.   No, no, no, not at all.
ZANIE.   Yes, thanks, thanks to you for all.
HERBERT.   No thanks to me at all.
           A very pleasant task, I ween,
           For both of us, my darling little queen.
BOTH.   'Tis joy, 'tis joy, etc.

HEPSICHORE. Zanie, wouldst know what is to befall thee on the morrow? Come hither, then, and thou shalt hear thy destiny.
ZANIE. Mother, and may I bring Herbert with me?
HEPSICHORE. As thou wilt, my child.

Enter FARRAL.

FARRAL. Thou hast chosen a romantic hour to unveil her future.
HEPSICHORE. The moon will be at the full to-night; she will be seen from every mountain top and from every green hill. The moon is a strange thing. and has more to do with our destiny than we ourselves know ; and in those soft and tender beams which she throws over every leaf and every sleeping flower. she has told me that on the morrow Zanie. my Zanie, shall be crowned our queen, and that she shall receive more respect than even the aged, because she is not of us, but above us. Give me your hand, Zanie. (*She looks at the lines on* ZANIE'S *hand.*) The moon has told me right. my child. Thy couch awaits thee ; go, thou, for the hour is late, and thou hast need of rest.   [*Exit* ZANIE.

No. 13. TRIO. HEPSICHORE, HERBERT AND FARRAL.

To thy silken couch away,
Gentle. gentle queen;
Balmy zephyrs round thee play,
Gentle. gentle queen:
Heav'nly visions of delight,
Cheer thy slumber all the night
'Till the rosy morning bright,
Gentle, gentle queen.

Dream of joy in store for thee,
Gentle, gentle queen,

Dream of what thou soon will be,
Gentle, gentle queen,
Happy visions, etc.

Slumber on, by fairies blest,
Gentle, gentle queen,
Fairies guard thy peaceful rest
Gentle, gentle queen,
Happy visions, etc.

While ZANIE *is sleeping,* HERBERT *steals cautiously towards her tent and sings.*

No. 14. SOLO.

Sleep, thou art happy, no cloud on thy brow,
I would I were dreaming as calmly as thou.
Thy thoughts o'er the future how lightly they roam,
While mine wander back to the dear ones at home.

CHORUS (INVISIBLE).

The dear ones at home, my own native home,
Oh, when shall I see them, the dear ones at home?

SOLO.

'Tis not that my friendship is waning for thee,
Oh, no! gentle maiden, that never can be,
But when I am gayest, sad moments will come
And carry me back to the dear ones at home.

CHORUS.

The dear ones at home, etc.

ZANIE. *waking, throws her mantle about her and goes to the opening of her tent (front).*

ZANIE. (*Spoken*) It is not well thus to indulge thy grief—
Yet not to chide or blame thee, do I speak,
But to console with kind and soothing words.
Go thou and sleep, and when thine eyelids close,
Thou shalt in dreams a message sweet, receive
From those who should be nearest to thy heart;
And on the morrow, if it shall be so,
That I am queen, then will I give thee wealth,
And high position, thou shalt have a place   •
Among the proudest in this realm of mine.

       [*Exit* HERBERT, *kissing his hand good-night.*

SCENE.—*Same as* SCENE VI.

No. 15. DUO.—TWO FLOWER GIRLS.

Up and away where the daisies grow,
Up and away where the glad streams flow,
Gather the wild flow'rs, wild and fair,
For our charming, lovely queen to wear;
Up and away where the lilies bloom,
Gather the rose with its sweet perfume,
Bind them with leaves from the evergreen,
For the snowy brow of our lovely queen.

The Gypsies assemble to witness the crowning of the Queen. ZANIE *is led forth arrayed in pure white, and seated on a pedestal decorated with flowers.*

FARRAL. *approaches and greets her respectfully. Then turning to the people he says in a loud, clear tone:*

" Behold her who is this day to be made our queen! The moon has said it, the stars have declared it, the breeze has whispered it in the ear of all the birds, and they are proclaiming it through the forest. Behold her, who is this day to be made our queen! Gather around her and pay her the court which becomes her rank!"

They all gather round her and sing.

No. 16. SOLO AND CHORUS.

SOLO.

Thou art purer than the lily,
Thou art fairer than the rose,
Thou art one of nature's children,
Every flower thy footstep knows.

CHORUS.

We are all thy willing subjects,
Hail our queen! all hail to thee!
For the golden stars have told us
Thine a happy reign will be.

SOLO.

How the gentle bubbling brooklet
To its merry song gives place,
While it mirrors on its bosom
Every feature of thy face.

CHORUS.

We are all thy willing subjects, etc.

SOLO.

Thou art winsome, kind and loving,
Good and true as thou art fair;
And the crown that soon will grace thee,
Thou dost well deserve to wear.

CHORUS.

We are all thy willing subjects, etc.

Enter MESSENGER *in great haste.*

MESSENGER. Our enemies, the house-dwellers, are upon us!
Sir Henry Glenville is at the head of a large party of men.
What 's to be done?

FARRAL. Let us defend ourselves to the last!

Enter SIR HENRY, MR. RINGGOLD (*father of* ZANIE), *and others,
with a simultaneous shout:*

"Hurrah, hurrah, hurrah! Thieves! Villains! Housebreak-
ers! Kidnappers! we have found you at last! We have come
fully armed, and it is needless for you to attempt any resistance!"

SIR HENRY. We are in search of two children. Give them
up, or we will demolish your tents and mow you down like
grasshoppers. (*Steps forward.*) There—there is my son!

MR. RINGGOLD. And I have every reason to believe that the
fair young girl that stands beside him is my daughter. We shall
see. (*He calls his wife, who is waiting outside.*)

Enter MRS. RINGGOLD, *singing the song with which she used to sing
her child to sleep.*

No. 17. CRADLE SONG.

1ST.

Sleep, my darling, gently sleep,
Angels bright their vigils keep;
Cradled on thy mother's breast.
Close thy laughing eyes and sleep.
Baby, sleep; darling, sleep;
Evening shadows round thee creep;
In its quiet, leafy nest,
Every bird has gone to rest.

ZANIE *starts and presses her hands to her head.*

2D.

Could I all thy future know,
Could I read its bliss or woe,
Will thy barque serenely glide
O'er a calm and silver tide!
Baby, sleep, etc.

ZANIE *soliloquizes*). What does this mean? I have heard that
song before.

3D.

Oh, how dear to me thou art,
Round the tendrils of my heart
Twining closer day by day,
Chasing every cloud away
Baby sleep, etc,

ZANIE (*continues to soliloquize*). Father! mother! Is it a dream
or a reality? That song has brought it all back to me. I remember one day, while playing in the garden, two rude men came:
one of them placed a handkerchief over my mouth and ran with
me as fast as he could.

MRS. RINGGOLD. I think she remembers. I'll call her by
her name. Isadore! my own darling!

ZANIE. That voice! that name! It is—it is my own dear
mother! (*She springs forward and they embrace.*)

MRS. RINGGOLD. And here is your father, Isadore.

ISADORE (ZANIE). Oh, father, I am so overjoyed! and it has
come so suddenly upon me that I scarcely know what to say.

MR. RINGGOLD. Well, my daughter, we shall leave these scenes
and return at once to our home in America. Come, friends, and
congratulate us upon the restoration of our children.

All go forward, HERBERT *going towards his father.*

HERBERT. First, papa, I must ask and receive your forgive-
ness. Do you blame me now?

SIR HENRY. No, my boy! I believe the hand of Providence
was in it all, and I most cheerfully and heartily forgive you.

STELLA (*approaching her brother and shaking his hand*). There,
Herbert! did I not tell you she was no gypsy girl?

ISADORE. Oh, papa, I never can be parted from Herbert! he
has been so kind to me, and has taught me so many things.

HERBERT (*to* ISADORE). And what need of our parting, my
darling little queen? You have long been the queen of my heart
and its affections, Isadore! will you not be mine ere you bid fare-
well to the green shores of Merry England? Promise it, dearest!
oh, promise it, or my future hopes will be wrecked forever!

ISADORE. I do promise it, with all my heart, providing you
can obtain the consent of our parents. First, go to my dear papa
and plead your own cause.

HERBERT. Thanks, my dear little queen! I'll do it at once.
(*To* MR. RINGGOLD:) Mr. Ringgold, I have long loved your
daughter Isadore, and I now come to ask her hand in marriage;
her heart she has already given me.

MR. RINGGOLD. Why, my boy, this is rather premature; but
since you have periled so much for my dear child, and you have
learned to regard each other with feelings of so tender a character,
I confess it would be unjust to cloud your young lives by a refusal
of a request to which I see no possible objection. What say you,
Sir Henry?

SIR HENRY. To what, Mr. Ringgold?

MR. RINGGOLD. To the union of these two young people, who
have been foolish enough to fall in love with each other.

SIR HENRY (*smiling good-naturedly*). I thought as much. But
come to my residence, where we can talk the matter over more
quietly.

*During the congratulations and the love-making the Gypsies availed
themselves of the opportunity of effecting their escape, and at the
close of the interview not a vestige of them was to be seen.*

MR. RINGGOLD. Why, what has become of the gypsies? Their
camp is deserted.

SiR HENRY. Well, let them go! they will give us no more trouble.

SCENE VII.—*The Drawing-room of the Mansion.*

Enter, the family and friends.

SiR HENRY. Now, friends, as we have had such a day of excitement, let us sit down quietly and enjoy ourselves during the little time which is left to us. Mr. Ringgold will leave with his family on the Ocean Queen to-morrow. Irene, let us have dinner at an early hour.

IRENE. Yes, father; I will give the order immediately.

MR. RINGGOLD. That is your eldest daughter, I presume, Sir Henry?

SiR HENRY. It is, and she supplies the place of her deceased mother.

MR. RINGGOLD (*to* SiR HENRY). Now, suppose we settle the question with regard to the marriage of our children. I, myself, should be proud of so excellent an alliance, and it only remains for you to give your consent, if you can do so consistently with your ideas of rank, &c.

SiR HENRY. Rank, in itself considered, has but little weight with me, compared with true dignity and real moral worth. If you deem my naughty, runaway boy worthy to become the husband of your lovely and amiable daughter, I have not the slightest objection to offer. On the contrary, I give my hearty consent to their union, which, if agreeable to you, shall take place at St. James' Chapel to-morrow morning at ten o'clock, to which we will invite our near relatives and friends.

MR. RINGGOLD. Let it be so.

ISADORE. Oh, thank you, thank you, papa! and you, Sir Henry! for you have made us so happy. (*To her mother:*) Come, mamma, give us your approval and your blessing.

MRS. RINGGOLD. I do, my darling. May Heaven bless you both!

At this point the dinner-bell is heard.

SiR HENRY. A very welcome sound that, judging from my own feelings, you must all be very hungry. Herbert, you and Isadore may lead the way.

[*Exeunt all, during which the March (No. 18) will be played.*

No. 18. ZANIE MARCH.

SCENE VIII.—*The Drawing-room of* SiR HENRY's *Mansion, decorated with flowers. Curtain rises on a company of friends of the family who have preceded the bridal party from the chapel to salute them with the Wedding Chorus. On the rising of the curtain the Chorus begins; immediately after the beginning of which, the bridal party enters.*

No. 19. WEDDING CHORUS.

Lo, they are coming with eyes beaming bright,
Sealed are the vows that their fond hearts unite,
Launched is their barque on a calm silver tide,
Joy to the bridegroom and joy to the bride;
Pure as the lilies we gather to-day,
Fair as the roses that bloom in their way,
Long may they glide o'er a calm silver tide,
Joy to the bridegroom and joy to the bride.

Though they are going to sail o'er the deep,
Angels around them their vigils will keep.
Friendship and mem'ry will sing as they glide,
Joy to the bridegroom and joy to the bride;
Joy to them both in the years that shall come,
Joy to them both in their far distant home,
Still may they glide o'er the calm silver tide,
Joy to the bridegroom and joy to the bride.

Here the married couple receive the congratulations of the company.

MR. RINGGOLD (*turning to* SiR HENRY). Well, Sir Henry, it is now time for us to prepare for our voyage, and once more, permit me to thank you for your many kindnesses and hospitality, and for the honor you have conferred upon me in giving me so noble and dutiful a son.

SiR HENRY (*to* MR. RINGGOLD). Don't mention it; you are more than welcome; and in return, let me thank you for the gift of a daughter who will be a bright ornament to the name she bears.

SiR HENRY (*to* HERBERT AND ISADORE). Children, God bless you! give you a pleasant voyage, and long, prosperous and happy life.

No. 20.

MR. RINGGOLD *sings.*

Good-bye, good-bye, the vessel waits
To bear us o'er the main,
And changes o'er us all may come,
Ere we shall meet again;
But true to friendship, true to love,
Our hearts will warmly beat,
And bright in mem'ry's urn will live
These happy hours so sweet.

SiR HENRY *sings.*

Yes, happy hours, but now the last
Comes stealing on apace,
And parting words must leave a shade
Of gloom on every face;
But let us hope that after years
Will glad reunion bring,
And we together may unite,
More joyful strains to sing.

DUO.—HERBERT AND ISADORE.

Say, why should sorrow cloud our brow,
Or tears at parting flow?
Two hearts at least are full of joy,
For you have made them so;
And now, good-bye, we must depart,
Soft blows the fav'ring wind,
God's blessing rest on us who go,
And you who stay behind.

FINALE.—CHORUS.

We'll keep this moment fresh and green,
And when at close of day
We sit us down to muse awhile,
Our thoughts to you will stray;
And zephyrs, as they come and go,
And fan each glowing cheek,
Will bring to us and bear to you
Each tender word we speak.
Farewell! farewell! &c.

CURTAIN.

"ZANIE."

INTRODUCTION TO OPERETTA. (POTPOURRI.)

2815–10

(3)

(9)

4

MET. ♩ = 112.
CANTABILE.

MET. ♩ = 69.

DELICATAMENTE.

Mет. ♩ = 104.

CON OSSERVANBA.

Мет. ♪ = 152.

ALLEGRETTO.

2815-10

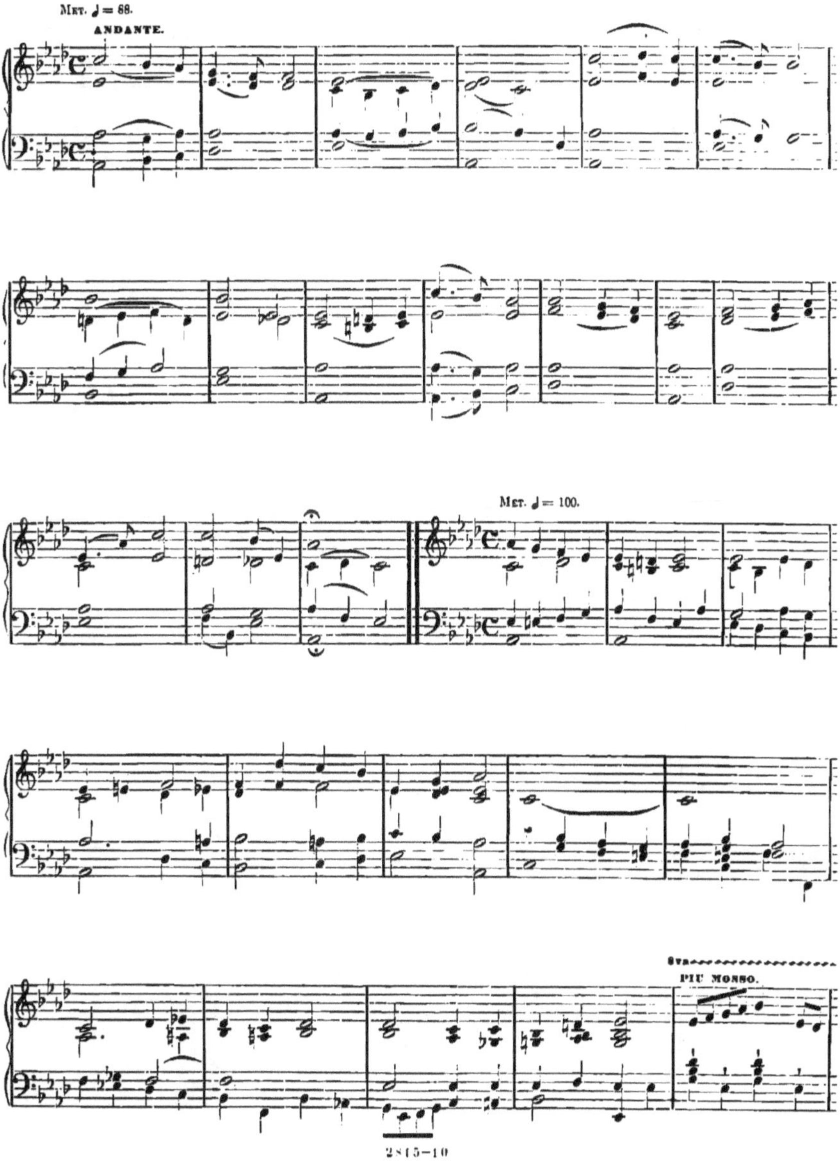
Met. ♩= 68.
ANDANTE.
Met. ♩= 100.
8va
PIU MOSSO.

8

Met. ♪ = 100.

MODERATO.

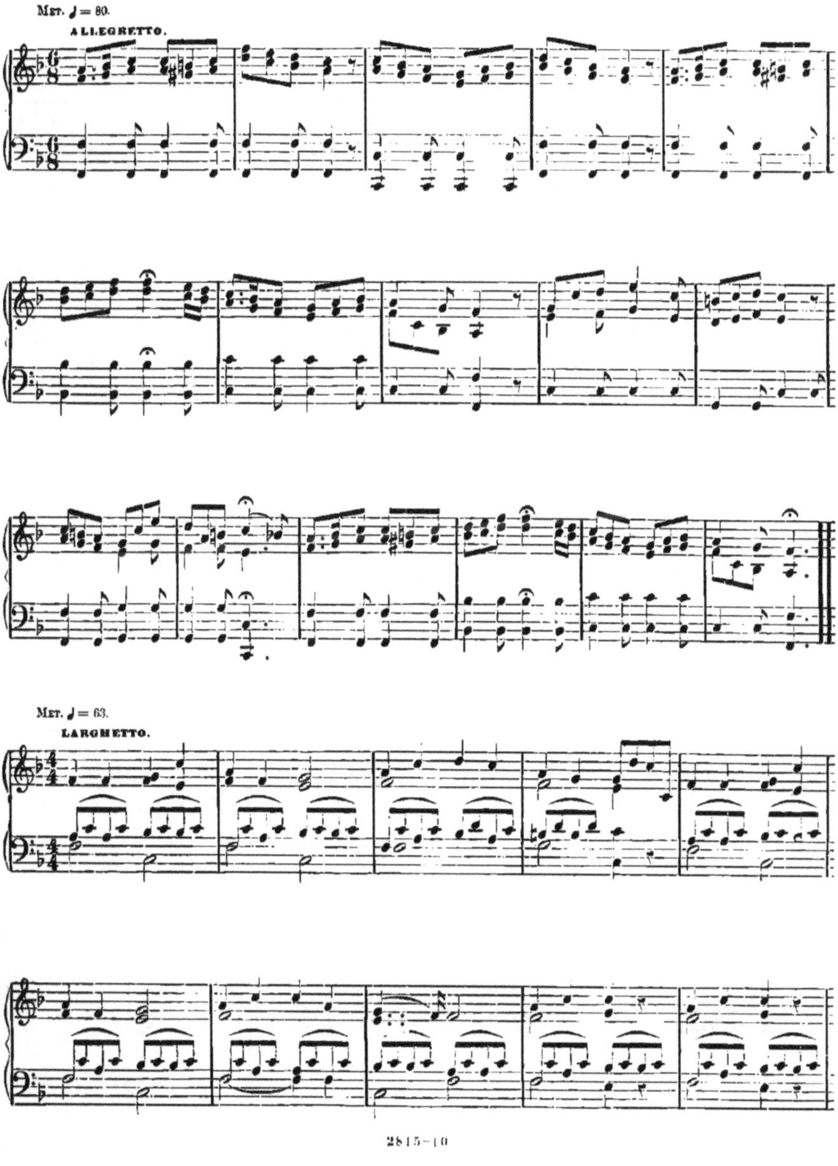
Met. ♩= 80.
ALLEGRETTO.
Met. ♩= 63.
LARGHETTO.

10

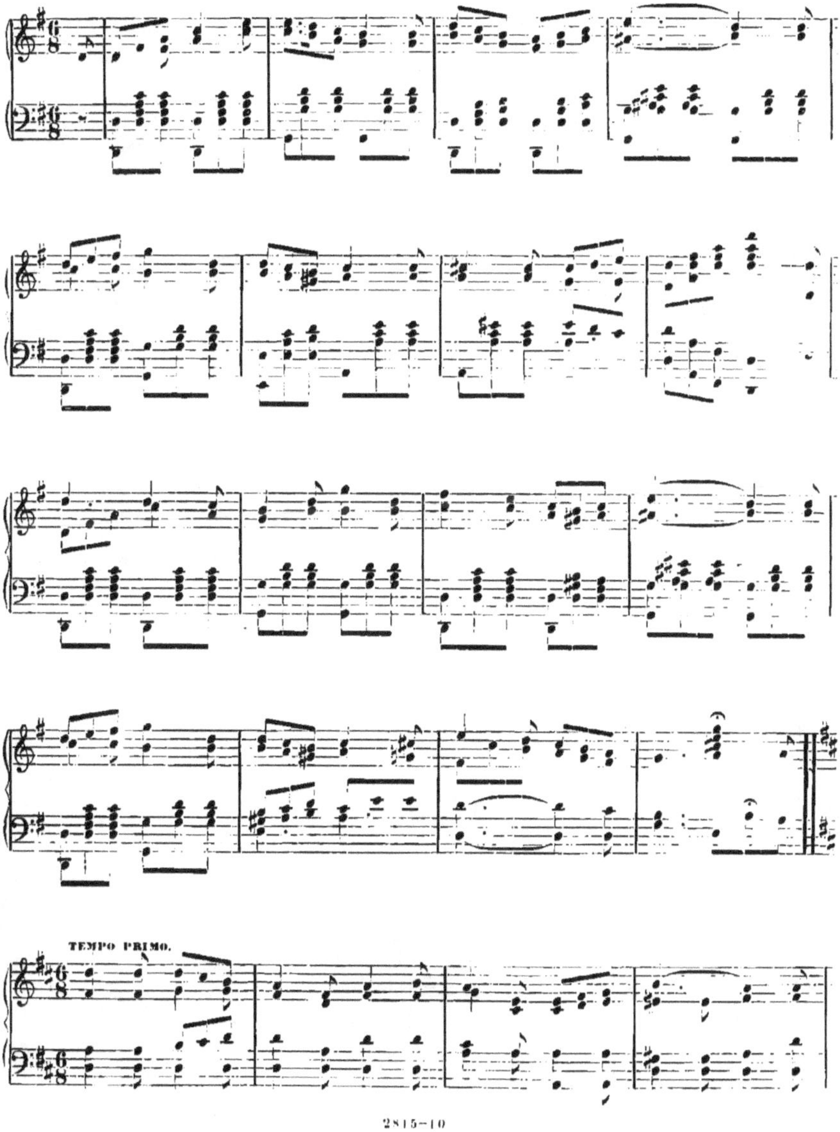
TEMPO PRIMO.

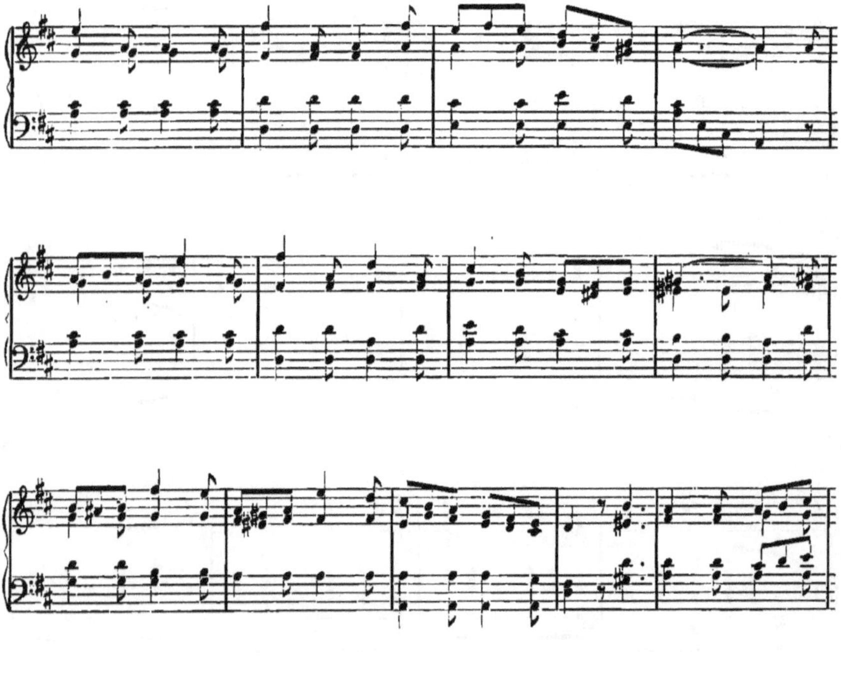
Ac - - - cel - - - - - - - - - - - - le - - - - - - ram - - - - - -
- - - - - - - - - do.

CHORUS OF GIPSYS.

1. The dew is on the snow-white thorn, The owl has gone to rest, And wan-ing stars are bear-ing hence The hours we love the

2. Bring forth, bring forth our graz-ing steeds, Let all be quick-ly done, For we must reach our dest-ined place Ere sets the gold-en

3. There's game for us and well we know,'Tis won by stealth and care, And he who best can play his part Will win the larg-est

2816—3

best; Now soars the lark on air - y wing To hail the op - 'ning day, Come, strike our tents with

sun; 'Tis gleam - ing o'er the mountain top With bright and gen - ial ray, Come, strike our tents with

share; Good-bye, good-bye, ye for - est wilds, And smil - ing vales so gay. Keep watch for us till

Last time omit. D.S.

live - ly hands, We gip - sys must a - way.

live - ly hands, We gip - sys must a - way.

our re - turn, We gip - sys must a-

D.S.

For last verse.

Accelerando.

way, We gip-sys must a way, a way, a way, a way,

way, We gip-sys must a-way, a way, a way, a way, a

Accelerando.

way, We gip-sys must a-way, a way, a way, a way, a

Accel.

way, a way.

way, a way.

way, a way.

WITH OUR FOOTSTEPS KEEPING TIME.

Solo and Chorus.

ALLEGRETTO.

No. 3.

SOLO. Soprano or Tenor. (A Gipsy.)

1. Now be - gins our night - ly rev - el, Now a - mid the dance we stand,
2. Let the mis - er count his treas - ure, Let the farm - er till the soil,
3. Hip, hur - rah, the moon is ris - ing, See, she comes our sports to grace,

Who so glad - some, free and mer - ry, As a rov - ing gip - sy band.
Yet to la - bor we are strang - ers, We were nev - er made for toil.
Peep - ing through the leaf - y branch - es With a mild ap - prov - ing face.

f CHORUS OF GIPSIES.

We will dance till high a - bove us Birds a - wake their ma - tin chime;

We will dance till high a - bove us Birds a - wake their ma - tin chime;

Ru - ral songs of mirth and pleas - ure With our foot - steps keep - ing time.

Ru - ral songs of mirth and pleas - ure With our foot - steps keep - ing time.

D.S.

YE ARE WELCOME, FRIENDS.

Solo.

DOLCE.

Zanie.

No. 4.

mf

1. Ye are
2. Ye are
3. Yes, a-

wel - come, friends, to our green-wood home, In the syl - van wilds, Where we love to roam. We have
wel - come, friends, to our fes - tal cheer, There is naught to harm, There is naught to fear, Then a-
way, a - way to the dance with me. I will bring you sweets From the hon - ey bee, I will

spread our feast 'neath the wail - ing trees, And our cheeks are fann'd by the laugh - ing breeze.
way, a - way to the dance to - night, Let your hearts be gay as your eyes are bright.
gath - er fruits that are rich and rare, And balm - y breath from the ros - es fair.

D.S.   Ending.

FLY, O BIRDLING.

Duo. Zanie and Herbert.

No. 5.

Fly, O bird-ling, do not stay.

Turn from gip-sy life a-way; You should learn to spell and read, Will you not my

coun-sel heed?   Take this prom-ise,

now, from me, If a gip-sy you will be. Then your coun-sel I will heed,

3

You shall teach me how to read.
Zanie.
I will be your faith - ful friend, On my word you may de - pend,
Herbert.
Will you be my faith - ful friend, May I on your word de - pend,
You shall find me ev - er true, What I prom - ise I will do.
Shall I find you ev - er true, What you prom - ise will you do?
8va

GOOD NIGHT.

Trio. Zanie, Stella and Herbert.

2820—2

And should we meet an · oth · er day, Our steps as light, our

And should we meet an · oth · er day, Our steps as light, our

hearts as gay. Oh, may our friend · ship strong · er grow, But now, good night, 'tis time to go.

hearts as gay. Oh, may our friend · ship strong · er grow, But now, good night, 'tis time to go.

A JOVIAL LIFE IS OURS.

Chorus of Male Voices.

ours, ha, ha! With lit-tle of trou-ble or sor-row, The clouds of to-day all van-ish a-way, And

world, ha, ha! As free as the zeph-yr a-bove us, We frown on the cold, but hon-or the bold, And bring us a brighter to - morrow, ha, ha! The proud may rest on their beds of down, But we, ev -'ry house-dweller

smile to the dear ones that love us, ha, ha! We watch the fields when the grain is ripe, We look on the reapers that

scorn - ing, Like birds on the wing we'll mer - ri - ly sing, And dance till the blush of the morning, ha, ha!

bind it, We stay not to plead, but take what we need, Wher-ev - er at midnight we find it, ha, ha!

TELL US, FAIRIES.

Chorus for Female Voices.

1. Oh, tell us, fai - ries, where you dwell, When win - ter winds are blow - ing, When
2. Oh, tell us, fai - ries, where you dwell, When snow - flakes crest the mount - ain. When

not a leaf is in the dell, Nor brook or rill are flow - ing? Where
syl - van chimes no long - er swell, And frost has sealed the fount - ain? Say,

2822-2

hide ye, then, oh, myst - ic train, In some bright star a - bove us, To

do ye plunge be - neath the waves In bells where moon - beams shin - ing, Re-

whis - per o'er the charm a - gain That binds to those that love us?

flect their light on co - ral caves, Where nymphs their wreaths are twin - ing?

WE COME FROM FAIRY-LAND.

Chorus of Fairies.

1. We come from fai - ry - land, And roam wher - e'er we will, We heed not win - ter's chill - ing storms, For

2. We scale the mount - ain's peak, And some - times in a star We float a - way at dew - y eve, To

we are hap - py still; We roam the earth, the air, And o'er the dist - ant

worlds un - seen a - far; When gen - tle spring re - turns, And may - bells sweet - ly

sea, We vis - it ev - 'ry sun - ny clime, Wher - e'er our thoughts would be.

ring, We seek the cool and shad - y grot, With for - est sprites we sing.

THINK OF THE ABSENT ONE.

Soprano Solo.

Mет. ♩ = 88.

ANDANTE.

mf Emily.

No. 10.

mf

1. Think of the ab-sent one,
2. Think of the ab-sent one,

gone from our sight, Think of the ab-sent one, roam-ing to-night,
where has he gone? Now at the ves-per time comes not his song;

Lone - ly the heart may be lad - en with care, Think of the ab - sent one,
Far from his place of birth, chance on the main, Bear him ye gen tle winds,

breathe him a pray'r.
home, home a - gain.

2824—1

NOW THE BURNING EMBERS GLOW.

Song of the Witch.

Met. ♩ = 100.

MARCATO.

mf Hepsichore. Mysteriously.

No. 11.

mf

mf

While the burn-ing em-bers glow,

In the cauldron now I throw, And to-geth-er stir them well. Drugs by whose mys-te-rious spell, Past and fu-ture

f Allegretto.

I can see, What has been and what will be; I to youth-ful lov-ers show Fate and for-tune,

Allegretto.

Cres.

bliss and woe; Now the ma-gic drugs u - nite,— Now the liquid drops are bright, the liquid drops are bright.

Cres.

2825—1

'TIS JOY, 'TIS JOY.

Zanie and Herbert.

4

read, to spell and read, My thanks to you for all, Yes, thanks to you for

No thanks to me at all, No

all, My thanks to you for all, Yes, thanks to you for all;

thanks at all, No, no, no, not at all, No thanks to me at all; A

ver - y pleas - ant task, I wean, For both of us, my dar - ling lit - tle

'Tis joy, 'tis joy to learn to spell and read, 'tis

queen. 'Tis joy, 'tis joy

joy to learn to spell and read, to learn to spell and read.

TO THY SILKEN COUCH AWAY.

Trio. Hepsichore, Herbert and Farral.

No. 13.

2827—2

Gen - tle, gen - tle queen; Hap - py vis - ions of de - light, Cheer thy slum - ber

Gen - tle, gen - tle queen; Hap - py vis - ions of de - light, Cheer thy slum - ber

Gen - tle gen - tle queen; Hap - py vis - ions of de - light, Cheer thy slum - ber

all the night, Till the ros - y morn - ing bright, Gen - tle, gen - tle queen.

all the night, Till the ros - y morn - ing bright, Gen - tle, gen - tle queen.

all the night. Till the ros - y morn - ing bright, Gen - tle, gen - tle queen.

2

SLEEP ON, THOU ART HAPPY.

Solo.

Met. ♪ = 100.

MODERATO.   Herbert.

No. 14.

1. Sleep on,   thou   art hap-py,   no
2. 'Tis   not   that   my friend-ship   is

cloud   on thy brow,   I would   I were dreaming   as   calm-ly   as   thou;   Thy thoughts o'er the
wan-ing   for thee,   Oh, no!   gen-tle maid-en,   that nev-er   can   be;   But when   I   am

fut-ure   how light-ly   they roam,   While mine wan-der back   to   the   dear   ones at home.
gay-est,   sad mo-ments will come,   And car-ry   me back   to   the   dear   ones at home.

2828—2

CHORUS OF GYPSIES.

The dear ones at home, my own native home, Oh, when shall I

The dear ones at home, my own native home, Oh, when shall I

see them, the dear ones at home?

see them, the dear ones at home?

UP, AND AWAY.

Duo.

Two Gipsy Flower Girls.

Up, and a - way where the dai - ses grow,

Up and a way where the glad streams flow, Gath - er the wild flow'rs

young and fair, For our charm - ing, love ly queen to wear.

Up and a - way where the

2829-3

li - lies bloom, Gath - er the rose with its sweet per - fume,

Bind them with leaves from the ev - er - green, For the snow - y brow of our

love - ly queen.

HAIL! OUR QUEEN, ALL HAIL.

Solo and Chorus.

48 3

CHORUS.

We are all thy will-ing sub-jects, Hail! our queen, all hail to thee! For the gold-en stars have

We are all thy will-ing sub-jects, Hail! our queen, all hail to thee! For the gold-en stars have

told us, Thine a hap-py reign will be.

told us, Thine a hap-py reign will be.

D.S.

2830-2

SLUMBER SONG.

1. Sleep, my dar - ling, gent - ly sleep, An - gels bright their vig - ils keep;
2. Could I all thy fu - ture know, Could I read its bliss or woe—
3. Oh, how dear to me thou art, 'Round the ten - drils of my heart;

Cra - dled on thy moth - er's breast, Close thy laugh - ing eyes and sleep.
Will thy barque se - cure - ly glide O'er a calm and sil - ver tide.
Twin - ing clos - er day by day, Chas - ing ev - 'ry cloud a - way,

2831—2

Ba - by sleep, Dar - ling sleep, Eve - ning sha - dows

'round thee creep; In its qui - et, leaf - y nest

Ev - 'ry bird has gone to rest.

D.S. Ending.

ZANIE MARCH.

From Danks' New Operetta, "Zanie."

H. P. DANKS.

TEMPO DI MARCIA.

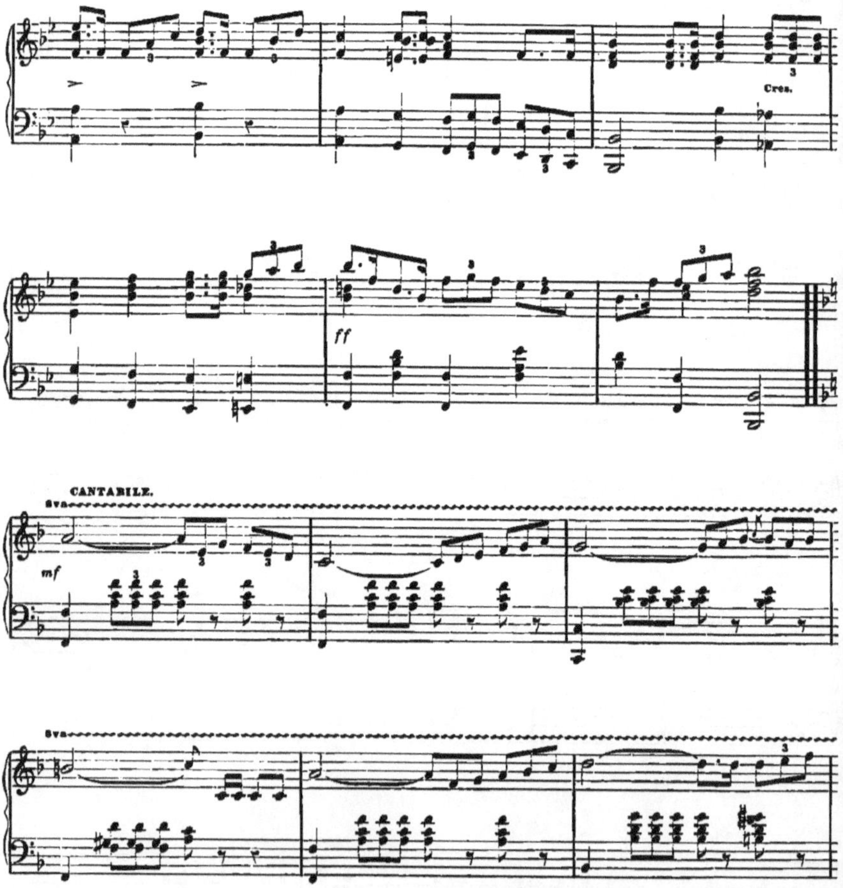
Cres.
ff
CANTABILE.
8va
mf

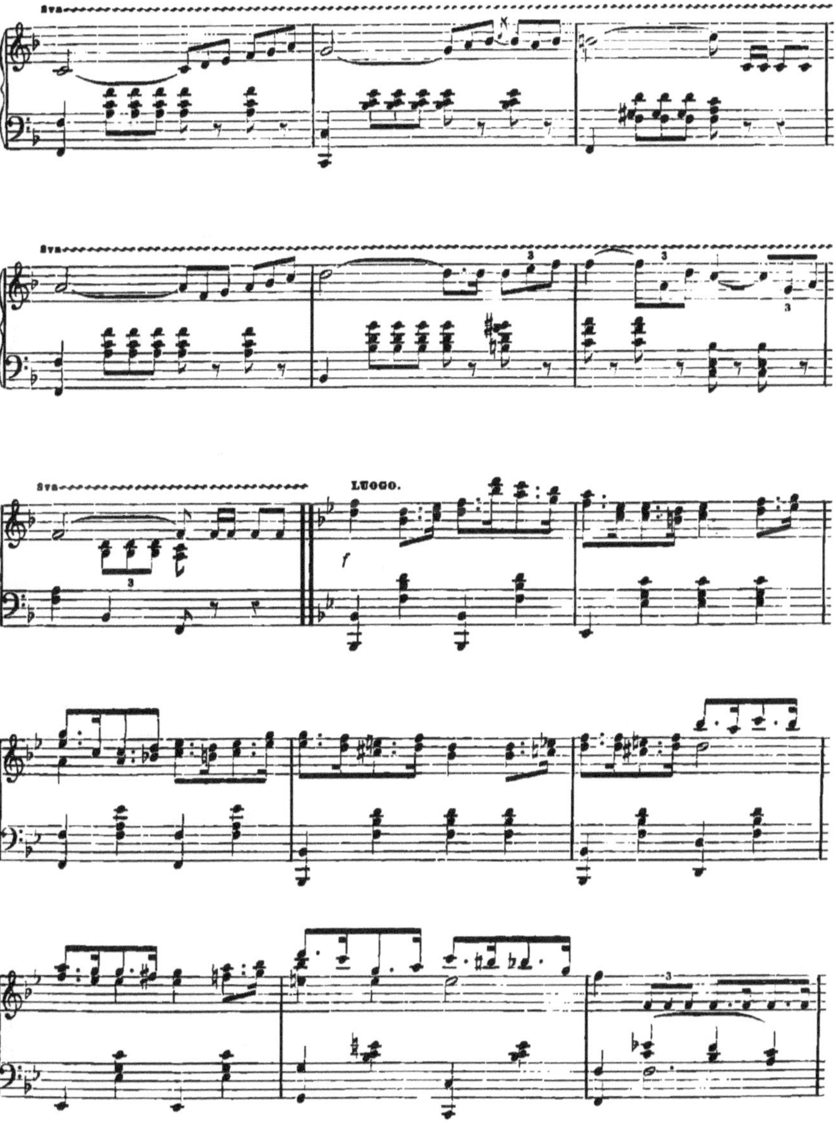
8va
8va
8va
LUOGO.
f
3

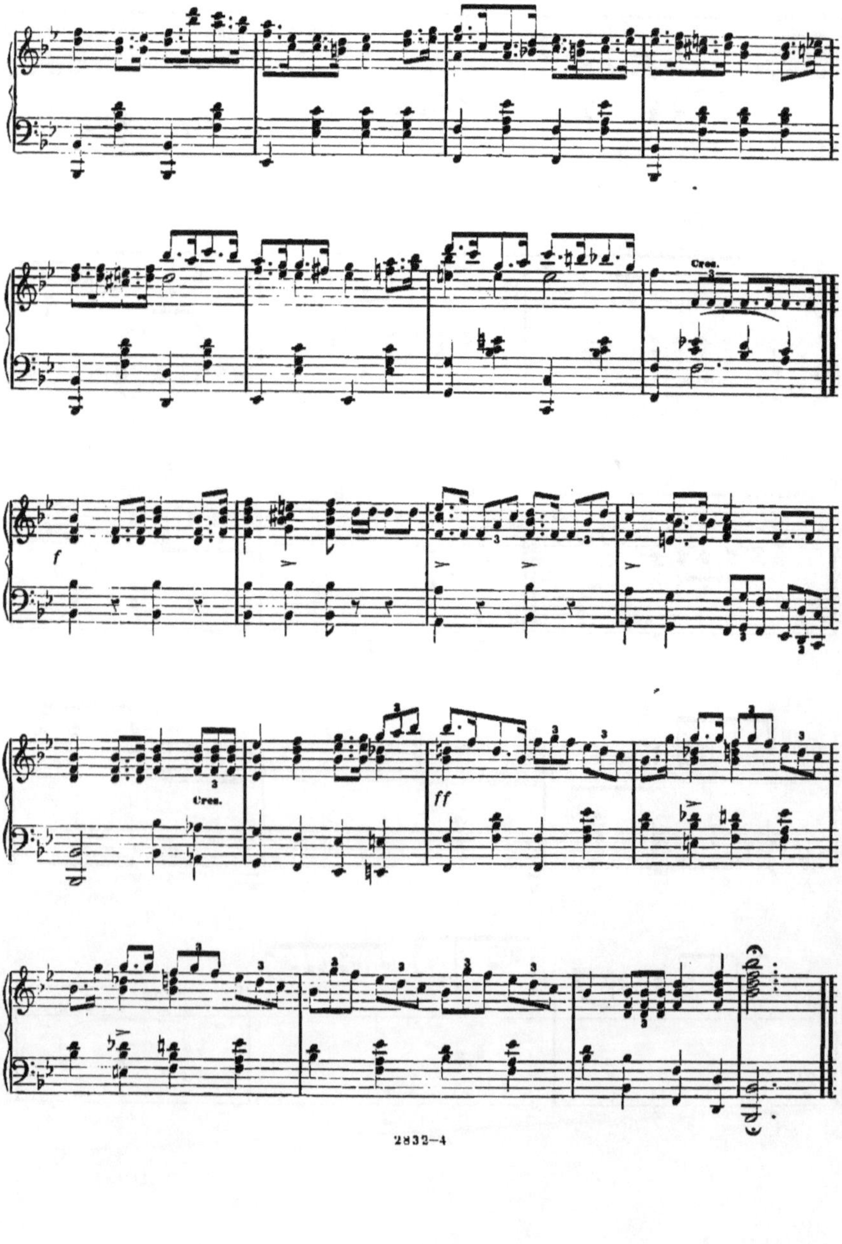
Cres.
f
Cres.
ff

WEDDING CHORUS.

ALLA MARCIA.

No. 19.

f

f Soprano.

1. Lo! they are com - ing with eyes beam - ing bright.

f Alto.

f Tenor.

2. Though they are go - ing to sail o'er the deep,

f Bass.

f

2833-3

Sealed are the vows that their fond hearts u - nite; Launched is their barque on a

An - gels a - round them their vig - ils will keep; Friend - ship and mem - 'ry will

calm sil - ver tide, Joy to the bride - groom, and joy to the bride.

sing as they glide, Joy to the bride - groom, and joy to the bride.

Pure as the li - lies we gath - er to - day, Fair as the ros - es that bloom in their way

Joy to them both in the years that shall come. Joy to them both in their far dist - ant home;

Long may they glide o'er a calm sil - ver tide, Joy to the bride-groom, and joy to the bride.

Still may they glide o'er the calm sil - ver tide, Joy to the bride-groom, and joy to the bride.

D.S.

FINALE.

Good bye, good bye, the ves - sel waits To bear us o'er the main, . . . And

chang - es o'er us all may come, Ere we shall meet a - gain; . . . But

2834—7

true to friend-ship, true to love, Our hearts will warm-ly beat, And

bright in mem-'ry's urn will live These hap-py hours so sweet,

Sir Henry Glenville.

Yes, hap-py hours, but now the last Comes steal-ing on a-pace, . . . And

2834-7

part - ing words must leave a shade Of gloom on ev - 'ry face; . But

let us hope that af - ter years Will glad re - un - ion bring, And we to - geth - er

may u - nite, More joy - ful strains to sing.

CON ALLEGREZZA.

Say, why should sor-row cloud our brow, Or tears at part-ing flow?. Two

hearts, at least, are full of joy, For you have made them so, . . And

now good bye, we must de-part, Soft blows the fav-'ring wind, . . God's bless - ing rest on us, who go, And you who stay be - hind.

CHORUS.

We'll keep this mo - ment fresh and green, And when, at close of day, We

We'll keep this mo - ment fresh and green, And when at close of day We sit us down to muse a - while, Our thoughts to you will stray; And

sit us down to muse a - while, Our thoughts to you will stray; And

zeph - yrs as they come and go, And fan each glow - ing cheek, Will

zeph - yrs as they come and go, And fan each glow - ing cheek, Will

bring to us and bear to you Each tender word we speak. Fare-well, fare-well, fare-
Fare - well, farewell, fare-
bring to us and bear to you Each ten - der word we speak. Fare - well, fare
well, fare - well, fare - well, fare - well!
well, fare well, oh, fare - well!
well, fare well, fare - well!